HOW TO DEVELOP STORY TENSION:

13 Techniques plus the Five Minute Magic Trick Guaranteed to
Keep Your Readers Turning Pages

HOW TO DEVELOP STORY TENSION:

13 Techniques plus the Five Minute Magic Trick Guaranteed to Keep Your Readers Turning Pages

By Amy Deardon

Taegais Publishing, LLC
sales@taegais.com
www.taegais.com

ISBN 978-1-940727-08-0 (print)

ISBN 978-1-940727-09-7 (ebook)

1 3 5 7 9 10 8 6 4 2

Printed in the United States of America

To *K*itty and *R*o,

Best Kids in the World!

I love you, Mom

Table of Contents

INTRODUCTION

You can write your novel with perfect sentences, and deliver heartbreakingly beautiful descriptions containing profound metaphors, but if you don't have tension in your story your reader is likely at any moment to put it down.

There are three fundamental reasons your story may not have tension:

1. The narrative does not have an Outer Story.

2. The narrative's story arrow from the Outer Story is not clearly articulated.

3. The narrative's story arrow is not moving forward.

This book explores practical methods, including an amazing five-minute trick, that you can use to automatically develop tension in your writing.

INNER AND OUTER STORY

Imagine that you're telling a quieter type of story, in which Justin needs to forgive his father, or Michelle wants to overcome an abused childhood. These are both strong internal conflicts. They're both good starts for a novel, but, sadly, by themselves not enough to form the novel. To do this, you need an external story line with a final tangible goal.

How do you add an external story line?

How about this: Justin and his wife move back to care for his ill father who is losing his house due to mistaken accounting. Justin must learn caretaking skills, and fight different battles including the main one with the state, and others with a realtor and with a neighbor. In the final climax, Justin first clears his father's name then forgives him, allowing the old man to die in peace.

Or this: Michelle decides to build a child-care center for foster abused kids. She is opposed by the lawyer of a powerful neighborhood group that doesn't want to lower the living standards. In the final climax, Michelle is able to overcome all problems to open the center.

In the midst of Justin's or Michelle's external battles, they also learn to overcome their inner struggles.

Story is comprised of two parts: the Inner Story, and the Outer Story. Both are necessary to have a resonant narrative.

Without an Inner Story the story moves from event to event, without exploration of the characters' emotional environment. A story like this might mechanically work—some action movies and books do this, as well as "puzzle" stories like Agatha Christie—but in general, without an Inner Story these generate disposable narratives.

On the other hand, without an Outer Story the narrative will die stillborn. You won't be able to finish your manuscript, or if you do it won't have a point to it.

To have tension you *must* have an Outer Story: external events occurring in the "real" story world and topping out at the climax and resolution. Imagine that you have a camera filming your characters. If they are drinking tea and reflecting on events, without moving through anything, you are not showing an Outer Story.

Many would-be authors I talk with are excited about writing a story, but too often what they describe is a premise—an interesting character, situation, or story world—without an actual external story to go along with this.

For more information on constructing the outer story progression, you can see my book *The Story Template*.

You can find a list of all Tips at the end of this book (XXpage 55). Here is Tip #1:

__Tip #1__: Make sure you include an external story line (Outer Story) in your narrative. The external line should include a Story Goal, Story Stakes, and Story Obstacles (to be discussed in a moment).

THE THREE STORY COMPONENTS

The Outer Story always consists of three general components: Story Goal, Story Stakes, and Story Obstacles. Let's look at these.

Story Goal

The Story Goal is the final overriding thing that your hero wants to accomplish in your story. For example, your hero may want to win the dance contest, or neutralize the terrorist (with as little life loss as possible), or find the treasure. You'll notice that these goals are quite specific and their attainment can be answered with a clear "yes" or "no." The Story Goal can be turned into the Story Question:

- WILL Rachel win the dance contest?

- WILL Nathan defeat the terrorist (and save the hostages)?

- WILL Mike be able to find the treasure?

———

Tip #2: *Make sure your Story Goal is specific, and preferably something physical. The Story Goal's attainment or lack thereof by the end of the story can be decisively answered with a "yes" or "no."*

———

Story Stakes

Your stakes explain why the story is important: if attaining the Story Goal isn't worthwhile, then your hero can just go home and laze around the pool. The Story Stakes must be important *to your hero*—even if your Story Stakes are minor in the scheme of things, they are critical for your hero, and your hero's desire causes your reader to also care.

Another point: your hero's motives for achieving the story goal are usually altruistic.

You can have multiple Story Stakes for a goal—emotional and physical both. For example:

• Rachel wants to win the dance contest so that she can use the prize money to pay for her sister's college education. She also wants to prove to herself that she has overcome her fear of being on stage.

• Nathan wants to win over the terrorist so that the terrorist will no longer hurt people, including the hostages the terrorist is now holding. Nathan also wants to prove to himself that even though he's older he's still relevant.

• Mike wants to find the treasure for historical interest—he would like to donate these priceless treasures to a museum so that many people can enjoy them.

———

Tip #3: *Make your Story Stakes important to your hero so they become important to your reader.*

———

Tip #4: *Your hero should want to accomplish something altruistic by achieving the Story Stakes.*

———

Story Obstacles

Story Obstacles are the main source of tension in your story, and therefore the main building block of your story. If your hero can automatically walk over and grab the Story Goal, there's no narrative. Obstacles fly furiously through the story, big and small, internal and external, quick solutions and tenacious problems.

Obstacles can be both internal and external. Internal obstacles are things like worry, fear, or lack of knowledge. External obstacles are things like people or terrain.

What is tension? The simplest definition might be that tension is the uncertainty of at least one element of your story. Story

Obstacles serve to put the outcome in doubt by blocking your hero's pathway to his goals.

———

Tip #5: *To maintain tension always keep at least one story element unknown or uncertain. Use internal and external Story Obstacles to keep the outcome of each action in doubt.*

13 TECHNIQUES TO INCREASE TENSION

*T*hese thirteen techniques, a Baker's Dozen, are great ways to increase tension in a sagging story. When you feel your story is dragging, or even if it isn't, consider how you can use one or more of these techniques to ratchet up your story.

An important point to remember is that every tension technique should leave your hero in a different, usually worse place than he was before. Watch out for the "One Darn Thing After Another Syndrome" in which there may be a lot of events, but ultimately they don't make a difference to your story.

———

__Tip #6__: Make sure every event that happens in your story puts your hero in a worse position than he was in before the event. Avoid the "One Darn Thing After Another Syndrome" in which your hero's story position is essentially unchanged after the particular event.

———

1. *Ticking Clock*

This technique is an oldie but goodie. Whether for large events or small, a time limit automatically ramps up tension.

Your hero is trying to do something hard. His story goal is hard, and the subgoal that he is currently trying to accomplish in this scene is also hard. By adding a time limit, you decrease the odds that he will be successful. Since your reader is rooting for your hero to win, she will naturally become more nervous, knowing how critical is this step and how likely your hero is to fail.

Example:

Joe is a starving lawyer. One day while helping an older lady load her groceries into her car (a "pet the puppy" action that is helpful to engender hero likeability), the older lady mentions wistfully that her husband used to help her. With this and that Joe grows suspicious that the husband died from poisoning due to toxic waste dumping from XYZ company. He decides to take on the company.

Since then a few things have happened in the story. In the current scene, Joe's subgoal is to retrieve a paper from the public defender's office and deliver it to the court.

To add a ticking clock, decide that the nefarious company suppressed releasing the deadline for filing this information until the last minute. Joe has only an hour to go all the way across town to get this information physically delivered to the court. Note that

Joe is not at fault for this late deadline—since you want to show that your hero is competent.

———

Tip #7: *A ticking clock is an amazingly effective way to add tension for actions both big and small.*

———

Tip #8: *Portray your hero as competent and likeable (he is funny, friendly, and performs "pet the puppy" actions in which he serves others).*

———

2. *Use a Mirror Character to Demonstrate Danger*

The mirror character in a story is someone who is similar to your hero: he may be pursuing the same general goal, or simply placed in a similar position (say, a fellow lawyer in the office). The mirror character demonstrates that a real threat exists to your hero, especially if he makes the wrong choice.

Example:

Joe our starving lawyer has a private investigator friend whom he hires to scope out dirt on XYZ company. Two nights later, Joe's friend calls him and says they have to meet. However, before they do Joe's friend drives his car off a cliff to his death.

__Tip #9__: A mirror character is someone similar to your hero, and can be used to demonstrate consequences of what may happen when the antagonist attacks someone. Often the harm occurs to the mirror character because he made a wrong choice.

———

3. _Make a Personal Threat_

Not only is the threat real, but directing it at your hero or (even better) those close to him makes the possible consequences even more worrisome.

Example:

Joe's wife comes home with a troubling story. At the post office with their two little boys, a man came up to her and said how sad it is when kids run into the street and are hit by a car. She wants to know what's going on, but Joe denies anything.

———

__Tip #10__: Real danger pointed at your hero or, better yet, those close to him, ramps up story tension.

———

4. *Take Away Something Important*

Your hero is trying to accomplish an almost impossible story goal. He will probably have friends and others helping him, and definitely will be using tools, knowledge, and other items to help him through the challenges. He is counting on these things!

What is a critical asset your hero has? Take it away.

Example:

Right before a big meeting with the judge in two hours Joe finds that his office is broken into and his car's tires are slashed. He has lost critical documents and his transportation. By not being able to successfully complete this meeting, he will incur penalties.

————

Tip #11: *On what is your hero relying—a person, information, a tool? Take it away!*

————

5. *Add a Character with a Conflicting Goal*

This technique works especially well when the additional character is an ally or an otherwise unexpected obstacle. A conflicting goal adds another layer of difficulty and doubt for your hero to accomplish his own goal.

Joe wants to go to Vermont to follow a lead investigating XYZ company. However, his wife is no dummy. Even though Joe hasn't told her what's going on, she's still shaken by that man in the post office and tells him she will not support his pursuing the case. They fight. She forbids him to go, or else she will take the boys and move back to Tennessee with her parents.

———

Tip #12: _Another character with a conflicting goal naturally opposes your hero. An effective means to ramp emotional tension is to make an ally into this oppositional character._

———

6. _Add a Positive for Not Completing the Goal_

This technique adds conflict within your hero so that he is split. Your hero may have two or more truly worthy options—he can check on A, or help B, or start preparations for C. Also, one of your hero's options may be a selfish one—your hero might be able to extricate himself from a painful situation by surrendering.

Example:

The head attorney from XYZ company meets with Joe and offers him a million dollar settlement if he will drop his case. Joe realizes the company is probably worried about a smoking gun somewhere, but darned if he knows what it is. Furthermore, Joe only has two days left before proceedings move to the next stage, so he doesn't have much more time to build his case. If Joe can't find more evidence, he and his clients are toast. And Joe's cut of that million dollars would sure come in handy.

———

Tip #13: Add a positive reason why your hero might not want to pursue his scene goal.

———

7. Close Options

Your hero starts pursuing his Story Goal with many options for action. Make sure you give consequences for each choice so that if he chooses a particular option, he will no longer be able to pursue the other good things he might have been able to do. These lost opportunities add to the tension because your hero's universe of choices is contracting. Your reader will bite her nails waiting to see what your hero decides.

Example:

If Joe agrees to a special meeting with the officials at the XYZ company, something that could be either helpful or not, he will no longer be able to file other requests.

———

Tip #14: Close your hero's options: if he chooses to do something, he will no longer be able to do an equally worthy alternative.

———

8. *Exploit the Unknown*

Even though you, the author, know the important twists of your story, your hero and reader don't. Delay revealing important information to ratchet up tension some more.

Example:

Joe has little time to prepare a trap for the opposing attorney. He texts his colleague that the attorney will be calling the colleague's cell phone in a few minutes, and Joe needs the colleague to answer with a particular coded greeting. Unbeknownst to Joe, though (you showed this scene previously), his colleague's wife borrowed her husband's cell phone for the day. Will the wife answer the phone as Joe instructed in the text?

———

Tip #15: Don't reveal all your cards for your story—generate suspense by letting your reader worry about unanswered questions.

———

9. *Make the Situation Worse than Previously Thought*

Tension builds when your reader learns that things are even worse than she had thought. You can either have your reader see an ominous scene of which your hero doesn't know (yet), or shock her along with your hero as he suddenly steps into empty space.

Example:

Joe looks into XYZ company's financial records. He discovers that the information he was counting on has been scrubbed. He doesn't know how he can possibly rebuild these links in time.

———

Tip #16: Reserve a bad surprise for your hero: something is worse than he thought it was.

———

10. *Throw in a Stunning Surprise*

A stunning surprise comes out of the blue to shock your hero and your reader. This is something he and she didn't see coming, and is usually a negative that immediately ramps up the danger and risk of failure for your hero as he goes about pursuing his story goal.

Example:

Joe wants to interview another victim of XYZ company's toxic poisoning. As Joe gets off the train to meet the victim, he sees a man he recognizes from the company, The man is coming fast and looks dangerous.

———

Tip #17: A bad surprise that stuns your hero is good for ramping up tension.

11. *Use Indirect or Confrontational Dialogue*

Dialogue in the novel is not the way real people talk—it has what is called "verisimilitude," or the appearance of reality. Dialogue, unlike real conversation, must always move efficiently as it heads toward a point.

Dialogue is a great place to include subtext—implying things that aren't directly said. Ironic statements can be dangerous or simply troublesome, and are fun to include.

Example:

~Joe and the opposing lawyer for XYZ company discuss a proposed agreement over a "friendly" cup of coffee~

Joe reached for his cup but then put it back on the table. He didn't want to be tempted to dump his coffee over Charles.

Charles smiled. His teeth glistened sharply. "Pretty straightforward, I think."

The agreement was too full of doublespeak, though. Joe doubted any court in the state would uphold it.

"I appreciate your work with this," Joe said. "I will discuss it with my clients, and get back to you soon."

Not likely.

————

Tip #18: Dialogue is not like real speech. Real speech is full of "umms," circling ideas, and pointless phrases (Hi, how are you? Good, and you?). Dialogue in fiction should contain the quality of verisimilitude—the appearance of reality—while remaining focused, efficient, and progressing through a specific (authorial) agenda.

————

Tip #19: Dialogue can contain great irony and indirect tensions that glue your reader to the story.

————

12. *Keep it Short*

Punchy sentences jar your reader, making her feel as if she, along with your hero, is being shaken. This technique can be used to highlight especially tense moments to drive home the anxiety.

Another way to keep it short is to use short chapters, especially for tense portions of your story. I serendipitously did this in my first novel and found the results amazing—so many people told me they wanted to get back to work or go to bed, but after a cliffhanger they peeked ahead to find the next chapter only had two pages. Alas, that one also ended on a cliffhanger, then another two page chapter…

Example:

"Get out now!"

Joe tensed.

Dave punched. Joe ducked under, then turned.

"I'm staying!" Joe shouted.

Dave punched again. Air. Joe spun and stepped back.

———

Tip #20: _Deliberately shortening your prose in tense scenes adds an extra punch to your words._

———

Tip #21: _Make your chapters short so they read quicker. This technique lures your reader to find out "just one more thing" in your story before taking a break._

———

13. *Keep the Problems Coming*

Remember the story of the old woman and the pig? Every time she thought she had her problem solved, another one appeared.

To prevent reader boredom, it's important to keep developing your story environment by solving old problems and adding new ones, rather than circling on the same old same old. When you heap more problems on your hero, mix them up so they're not all of the same type. Some should be physical, some logistical, some with other people.

The trick to adding problems is that your hero must be in a worse place than before after each problem appears. Watch out for the "One Darn Thing After Another" Syndrome in which the hero stays stuck dealing with things that don't essentially change his circumstances. "The Old Woman and Her Pig" arguably falls into this category, although it so clearly illustrates the importance of adding obstacles that I've included it here.

Example:

THE OLD WOMAN AND HER PIG

Once upon a time an old woman was sweeping her little house, when, to her great joy, she found a silver sixpence.

"What," said she, "shall I do with this little sixpence? I think I will go to market and buy a pig." So the next day she went to market and bought a nice little white pig. She tied a string to one of the pig's legs and began to drive him home.

On the way the old woman and her pig came to a stile, and she said:

"Please, pig, get over the stile."

But the pig would not.

Just then a little dog came trotting up, and the old woman said to him:

"Dog, dog, bite pig;

Pig won't get over the stile,

And I sha'n't get home to-night."

But the dog would not. So the old woman held up her stick, and said:

"Stick, stick, beat dog;

Dog won't bite pig;

Pig won't get over the stile,

And I sha'n't get home to-night."

But the stick would not.

So the old woman gathered some bits of wood together to make a fire, and set them on fire, and then threw her stick into the fire and said:

"Fire, fire, burn stick;

Stick won't beat dog;

Dog won't bite pig;

Pig won't get over the stile,

And I sha'n't get home to-night."

But the fire would not.

So the old woman fetched a pail of water that was standing near and said:

"Water, water, quench fire;

Fire won't burn stick;

Stick won't beat dog;

Dog won't bite pig;

Pig won't get over the stile,

And I sha'n't get home to-night."

But the water would not.

Then the old woman saw an ox coming; so she said:

"Ox, ox, drink water;

Water won't quench fire;

Fire won't bum stick;

Stick won't beat dog;

Dog won't bite pig;

Pig won't go;

I see by the moonlight

It's long past midnight;

Time pig and I were home an hour and a half ago."

But the ox would not.

So the old woman turned around and saw a butcher, and she said:

"Butcher, butcher, kill ox;

Ox won't drink water;

Water won't quench fire;

Fire won't burn stick;

Stick won't beat dog;

Dog won't bite pig;

Pig won't go.

I see by the moonlight

It's long past midnight;

Time pig and I were home an hour and a half ago."

But the butcher would not.

So the old woman took a rope out of her pocket, and said:

"Rope, rope, hang butcher;

Butcher won't kill ox;

Ox won't drink water;

Water won't quench fire;

Fire won't burn stick;

Stick won't beat dog;

Dog won't bite pig;

Pig won't go.

I see by the moonlight

It's long past midnight;

Time pig and I were home an hour and a half ago."

But the rope would not.

Just then a large brown mouse ran across the meadow, and she said:

"Mouse, mouse, gnaw rope;

Rope won't hang butcher;

Butcher won't kill ox;

Ox won't drink water;

Water won't quench fire;

Fire won't burn stick;

"Stick won't beat dog;

Dog won't bite pig;

Pig won't go.

I see by the moonlight

It's long past midnight;

Time pig and I were home an hour and a half ago."

"Yes," said the mouse, "I will, if you will give me some cheese."

So the old woman put her hand in her pocket and found a nice piece of cheese; and when the mouse had eaten it:

The mouse began to gnaw the rope,

The rope began to hang the butcher,

The butcher began to kill the ox,

The ox began to drink the water,

The water began to quench the fire,

The fire began to burn the stick,

The stick began to beat the dog,

The dog began to bite the pig,

And the pig began to go.

But what time the old woman and her pig got home neither you, nor I, nor anybody knows.

— *Tales of Laughter* (1902), eds. Kate Douglas Wiggin and Nora Archibald Smith

———

Tip #22: Most of the Outer Story is a series of actions and reactions—a problem is solved, and another takes its place. To push the story arrow forward, you need to constantly add new problems so your hero's quest to solve his story goal brings constant change and enlightenment. Make the Story Obstacles of different kinds: a need to escape a location for one, a logistical problem, and then an emotional confrontation. Remember that the solution of each Story Obstacle should leave your hero in a different, usually worse place than when he started.

THE FIVE MINUTE TRICK TO DEVELOP STORY TENSION

*T*he story is made of two main branches:

The Inner Story: the emotional journey your hero takes that teaches him an important lesson about how to live.

The Outer Story: the physical events that occur in the "real" story world.

Many manuscripts I critique have what I call "meandering story" that takes place in the Outer Story. While the Outer Story may be showing lots of action, it's not gripping because the events described are irrelevant to story progression. In other words, the story is not developing (no forward story arrow).

———

__Tip #23__: To prevent Meandering Story you need to make sure that all the actions in your story, and especially your Outer Story, are building upon and leading to something. Include all the steps you need, and eliminate the side trails.

———

Scene and Sequel

*T*he Scene-and-Sequel construction was first described (to my knowledge) by Dwight Swain in his 1965 book *Techniques of the Selling Writer*, which has since undergone multiple reprints. Other writers have subsequently described this technique including Jack Bickham in his 1999 book *Scene and Structure*, which is where I learned about it.

This is a powerful technique! It's straightforward and not difficult to master. By using it you will direct your writing events to always be focused and forward-moving.

Writing with the Scene and Sequel assumes that you are writing in first person (I, me) or 3rd person limited, in which you describe what only one character at a time experiences.

Briefly, the story can be broken into Scenes and Sequels. The scene describes the outward action of your story—what a camera would pick up if it were filming your narrative. The sequel describes the inner reaction one of your characters has to the previous scene.

———

Tip #24: The novel is made up of beads of Scene-Sequel-Scene-Sequel from beginning to end. The purpose of the scene is to clearly articulate the outer story action so that your reader can easily follow story events. The sequel serves to describe your characters' inner emotions and thus increase reader bonding with them and with your story outcome.

THE SCENE

*H*ow many scenes are there in a novel? While scene number is variable depending on length of each scene and length of the manuscript, a good guestimate for number of scenes might be about 50-100. Remember that more shorter scenes is better than fewer longer scenes for generating tension because shorter makes the words and story seem to move faster. One reason for the seeming speed is that shorter disallows rabbit trails and extraneous verbiage that slow a story. That being said, include what you need to include.

Each scene needs a reason to be included in your story. The scene must advance your novel in some way—your story moves because of your scene. In other words, your hero has an additional problem to solve, or your antagonist has succeeded with a task, or an important character is now missing. Don't just have your characters pointlessly talking or walking around.

The Scene can be divided into three distinct parts:

• Goal

• Conflict

• Disaster

———

Tip #25: Each scene must have a purpose and must advance your story in some way. Avoid pointless events, excess verbiage, explanations, background, and rabbit trails.

Point of View

*E*ach scene is told from the point of view (POV) of one and only one character. This means that all things observed, recorded, and felt internally are experienced only by your POV character. You may change POV characters as you write different scenes, but POV within the scene must remain rock-solid.

If you have trouble writing from only one character's viewpoint, simply write the scene in the first person—I did this, I saw that. When you're finished, replace the "I's" with your character's name.

To choose which POV you want to use for your scene, ask yourself:

• Who is most affected by the scene's events?

• Who has the most insight into these events?

• Alternatively, who will not understand the events, although your reader will? This is sometimes a fun trick to use.

If you're not sure with whom you want to stick for the scene, try writing it from more than one POV to determine who might be the best character to tell this part of your story.

———

Tip #26: *Each scene can only be told through one character's point of view (POV). All observations and emotions in one scene are from the perspective of your POV character. You may switch POV characters for different scenes.*

Goal

*F*or each scene you must formulate a specific, extrinsic goal that will be clearly attained, or not attained. This goal must be important to your hero (stakes).

For example, suppose your hero needs to clear his friend's reputation, since his friend has been wrongly accused of something. Then this scene's goal might be to retrieve an exculpatory paper from the bad guy's desk.

This goal must be clearly stated in one sentence at the beginning of the scene. For example, you could open your scene by writing:

Tom had to find the paper that would prove Evan was innocent, and he only had ten minutes before George would return.

Did you notice the ticking clock? These are always fun to include.

This sentence may sound too obvious for your reader, but trust me, it isn't. Remember that you need to be crystal clear when articulating what is going on in your Outer Story. Leave the interpretation and innuendo for the emotional and thematic parts.

———

Tip #27: *The Inner Story interprets emotions and "inner journeys" and can well tolerate indirect statements and ironic or unstated conclusions. In contrast, the Outer Story statements describing action in story events should be unambiguous since the Outer Story is the framework for everything else.*

Tip #28: *State your scene goal or scene question in one sentence, and use it to start your scene. This goal must be answered clearly with a "yes" or "no" by the end of the scene.*

———

Conflict

The conflict takes the major proportion of your scene. This is the back-and-forth interplay that is so compelling for your reader because it prolongs the uncertainty of how the scene goal will be answered.

Conflict occurs when your hero encounters obstacles to fulfilling his scene goal. These obstacles can be internal or external.

Internal obstacles are things like fear and lack of knowledge.

External obstacles are things like people or terrain.

Scenes usually have about four obstacles that are both internal and external types. The good news is that stories typically deal with one obstacle at a time. This means you don't have to do complicated interweaving of problems as you go to answer the scene question—just solve one obstacle, then move onto the next.

If you wish to increase tension, you may want to quickly list some hero-known obstacles at the beginning.

For example, you might write:

Tom had to find the paper that would prove Evan was innocent, and he only had ten minutes before George would return.

Tom knew that George might have a pressure alarm in the desk, but he'd worry about that when he got there. First, he had to get through the door.

The door was the old-fashioned kind, with a heavy turn lock. He'd have to rig a way to catch the latch. Tom dug in his pocket, looking for the slim piece of metal he'd grabbed earlier...

Make sure that your obstacles represent real dangers that grow naturally from your story and aren't silly. One of my favorite demonstrations of a non-real threat is the Hydra from the 1963 film *Jason and the Argonauts*. I encourage you to look up this five minute sequence on youtube; it is a great cautionary visual.

I call this sequence the "Welfare Hydra." Watch the clip, then tell me what this Hydra is actually doing?

Yes, he looks theatening with his multiple heads slithering near Jason. You can almost hear the Hydra squeaking, "I'm scary! I'm scary! See how scary I am?" But does the Hydra actually attack Jason? Does he even approach him? Umm, no.

———

Tip #29: Scene Conflict takes up the major part of your scene. It features your hero striving for his Scene Goal while being held back by obstacles. Scene Obstacles can be both internal and external.

Tip #30: Scene Obstacles are usually answered sequentially, not interwoven. This makes writing the scene easier.

———

Tip #31: If you wish to increase tension, you may list some hero-known obstacles at the beginning of your scene before your hero starts sequentially dealing with them.

———

Tip #32: Make sure you're not adding Obstacles simply to add Obstacles. They need to be real problems that take ingenuity to solve. This is what makes story fun.

———

Disaster

You need to answer your scene question at the end of the scene. Remember that tension means the uncertainty of at least one element—so when you answer the scene question, you must also raise another uncertainty. This technique pulls your reader along from scene question to scene question.

To introduce uncertainty while answering your scene question, you must answer by either:

- Yes, But…

- No, and Furthermore…

The YES, BUT answer gives an affirmative, but a negative consequence as well. For example, in our scene question: Will Tom find the paper in time? You answer it: YES Tom finds the paper, BUT Cathy sees him take it. This leads to the next scene question: Will Tom be able to convince Cathy not to tell George about taking the paper?

The NO, AND FURTHERMORE answer makes the situation even worse. For example, you ask: Will Tom find the paper in time? You answer it, NO Tom doesn't find the paper, AND FURTHERMORE he triggers an alarm on George's desk that alerts the police to arrest Evan. This leads to your next scene question: Will Tom be able to warn Evan to get away before the police arrive?

Notice that Tom caused the bad results and next scene question in both examples. Don't have bad things fall out of the sky; make them consequences of actions.

——

Tip #33: You must answer your scene question, but in such a way that the answer leads to a new scene question. The "Yes, But" answer gives an affirmative, but also a negative consequence. The "No, and Furthermore" answer tells your reader your hero failed in his scene goal, and this failure has made his situation even worse.

——

Tip #34: Make sure the new scene goals are the result of your hero's actions or another cause you have previously set up. Bad things should not just fall from the sky.

THE SEQUEL

*T*he sequel is easy to forget including because it's quiet and quick. However, without the Sequel you will not create reader bonding with your characters—your reader will be on the outside and uninvolved as she watches your story. She won't care what happens because she won't care about your characters.

The sequel describes your character's internal reaction to the last scene's disaster. The sequel can be short—only a line—or an entire section itself.

Like the scene, the full-blown sequel takes place in a stereotyped sequence. Although the novel usually intersperses sequel reactions within the scene, and usually truncates sequels at the end of the scene, it's important to go through the process just so you understand where is your character after an event. This sequel order is easy to remember because it's logical.

——

Tip #35: The Sequel brings your reader emotionally closer to your characters by having her understand what they think and how they react to story events. Sequel can be one line or full-blown. These are easy to forget to include, so make sure you have them.

Emotion

The emotion portion of Sequel describes your hero's emotional reaction to the previous scene's disaster: fear, anger, worry, grief, or whatever.

For example, Tom's disastrous search for the paper in George's desk leaves him anxious that he's going to be caught in the next few minutes.

––––

Tip #36: When your character breaks away after a Scene Disaster, the first thing he does is to emotionally react to the stunning bad news. These emotions aren't logical, simply felt. Some common ones are fear, anger, worry, or grief.

––––

Thought

After your hero calms himself, he looks at his options. An effective technique is to use the dilemma—two (or more) choices, all bad. Have your hero consider each choice and articulate the good and bad consequences of each potential action.

For example, Tom might decide he has three options. 1. He can pretend his being in George's office was due to a wrong turn and hope Cathy doesn't follow up to tell George. This tactic wouldn't work because Cathy probably knows George keeps his door locked. 2. He can let the chips fall where they may and just get out of there. This would certainly lead to a bad outcome where his cover is blown. 3. If Tom can convince Cathy to come with him, he can show her his evidence and hope she switches to his side. The negative is her absence might trigger a red flag to George.

––––

Tip #37: After your hero deals with emotions, he must determine his options. List them clearly, with pros and cons for each one. Try to introduce two or more bad options, with no good ones.

––––

Decision

Your hero must decide what he's going to do. This decision needs to be clearly stated, either here and/or at the beginning of the next scene. The cliffhanger tempts your reader to "read just one more chapter" to answer the question you've just planted.

For example, Tom decides to take Cathy with him if he can, since she could be a powerful ally.

––––

Tip #38: After clearly reflecting on all his options, your hero should state his decision in one clear sentence. This statement goes either at the end of the sequel, and/or at the beginning of the next scene.

Action

Your hero moves to take the first action of his decision. This fourth part is often not present in the sequel, but waits for the start of the next scene.

For example, Tom has decided to try to get Cathy to come with him. His first mini-goal is to convince her to come with him.

"I'm looking for a particular paper," Tom said. "Can I show you why? It'll just take an hour or two."

Tom noticed Cathy's mouth tighten. Then she nodded.

(The next scene goal might be, then, to get out of the house together unnoticed by the guards).

———

Tip #39: After stating his decision, your hero figures out the first thing he needs to do to take action. This start-of-action may be at the very end of your sequel, or at the start of your next scene.

PUTTING IT INTO ACTION

Yea! Finally, you're ready to go ahead to implement this Scene-Sequel technique. This technique works to generate tension because it clearly and automatically directs your story arrow forward. Your reader can easily follow your story to understand what is going on and emotionally bond with your characters. Even though your reader probably won't consciously recognize this structure, she will definitely respond positively.

Taking five minutes to preplan each scene and sequel before you start writing will also eliminate writer's block.

———

Tip #40: *By taking five minutes before writing each scene or sequel to clearly articulate why you're including it and where it is headed, you will automatically generate a powerful forward story arrow that your reader will love.*

———

Tip #41: *To write your scene, include the following small outline at the top of your blank page:*

POV:

GOAL:

CONFLICT:

DISASTER:

__Tip #42__: To write your sequel, include the following small outline at the top of your blank page:

POV:

EMOTION;

THOUGHT;

DECISION:

ACTION:

Even if you don't write a long sequel, it's helpful to do this exercise so you can understand how your characters are responding to your story events.

EXAMPLE OF THE SCENE-SEQUEL TECHNIQUE

You can walk with me as I put this scene-sequel technique into operation. The following is a chapter from my book, *A Lever Long Enough*.

Here's the background:

This part of the story takes place in an Israeli military complex in the pseudo-present time. It is the middle of the night. An event in the lockdown for prisoners has just occurred, in which a prisoner was killed and a security guard injured and in a coma. Since a time machine mission in the complex is ongoing, the base is sealed from anyone going in or out.

Aaron is in charge of security and determined to evacuate the guard to a hospital where he can receive best treatment and hopefully soon awake and be questioned. He suspects Gideon, who is second in command of the complex and was present at the event, of being a traitor. Gideon does not want the soldier evacuated. Both Aaron and Gideon are waiting for Landau, the base commander, to arrive so they can make a decision. Feinan, discussed in the conversation, is Benjamin Feinan who is leading the mission in the past.

————

From my notes here's the SCENE OUTLINE:

POV: Aaron

GOAL: Cat-and-mouse to slip up Gideon and get him to admit to something—he will catch this spider in its lair.

CONFLICT: Gideon is cool and obviously too smart to slip. Once Landau arrives Aaron wants to convince Landau to evacuate the soldier, but he will have to argue hard against Gideon. He's frustrated because he won't be able to convince Landau that Gideon is dangerous; Gideon, a decorated soldier, battle leader, and second in command of the complex is the last person Landau would suspect of treason.

Internally Aaron's dealing with fatigue, frustrated suspicion, and worry that the mission will fail.

DISASTER: Gideon wants to talk alone with Landau, and Aaron realizes Landau is extremely vulnerable to harm (either physical or hearing suspicions about Aaron). Yet there is nothing he can do to protect Landau.

Next scene goal: Convince Landau to lift the seal and evacuate the soldier.

NOTE: You'll note that sequel emotions and thoughts (analysis) are interspersed throughout the scene event developments. There is a truncated sequel at the end, in which Aaron's immediate plan is to open Landau's door to keep him as safe as possible, and then to set up the conference room for his visual displays of the lockdown event.

✳

Aaron peeped in Gideon's office and saw him seated behind the desk, his cigarette glowing like a ruby eye in the darkened room.

"Reuven," Gideon said to Aaron. "Come in if you'd like."

The suite of offices was deserted at three thirty in the morning, the big room leading to the individual doors off lit with foot-level lights. Gideon's was the only door open, and Aaron smiled as he stepped inside. He'd catch this spider in its lair.

The tip of the cigarette grew bright red as Gideon inhaled.

"Cigarette?"

Aaron hesitated, took one, and Gideon slid his pocket lighter across the desk.

The smoke was sharp but not unpleasant in his lungs, hot, and as he breathed in again he drifted into the cold awareness of the chase.

"How's your man?" Gideon asked.

Aaron rolled the cigarette between his fingers for a moment before answering. "Stable. He's unconscious. The doctor says he needs an MRI and some specialized drugs we don't have here. He needs to be moved out."

"Mmm." Gideon breathed against his cigarette. "No one likes losing soldiers under their command, but these things happen."

"He's not lost. The doctor holds out good hope for him if he can be transported."

"One man isn't worth the mission. We can't lift the seal over the base."

Aaron bit back a retort, then tapped his cigarette against the ashtray on the desk. He'd broken the habit years ago but all the little motions of smoking came back so easily.

The base commander was due in ten minutes.

There was dark smoke in his lungs.

Gideon sat forward and ground the end of his cigarette into the ashtray. Ashes flickered and went black.

"I lost men in ReachDeep," Gideon went on, almost as though he were talking to himself. "Four years, thirteen operations, twenty two men. It's never easy."

Aaron steepled his fingers together, and nodded.

Gideon went on. "Horrible deaths I've seen, and afterwards. The bodies of two of my soldiers were dragged through the street, spat on, torn apart. Another body was tripped with mines so we couldn't retrieve and bury it. He rotted in the open, with just a poor shelter we built over him to keep the wild animals away. After awhile—"

He shook his head.

Aaron snuffed his cigarette.

Gideon sighed. "I'll tell you who has nine lives."

"Who?"

"Feinan. Extraordinary. He went into situations that were nigh impossible; not only came out but always successful. Hostage rescue, mostly. I swear soldiers jumped in front of bullets for him. He was called the "Viper" by the Palestinians."

"I know."

Gideon leaned forward to reach for another cigarette. Aaron pushed the pack and the lighter toward him across the desk. His face was in shadow, he knew. Sometimes that helped people to talk.

For a moment, the bright orange flame illuminated Gideon's face. Dark shadows under his eyes. His cigarette glowed.

"He had a bounty on him," Gideon said. "A king's ransom. They almost got him too: that car bomb when his wife died four years ago. He's never been the same. But still dangerous. Very dangerous."

"How did they know where to plant the bomb?"

Gideon shook his head. "Someone close to him might have leaked the information, but they never found who. All that money."

Aaron wasn't sure, but he thought he saw Gideon smile. Aaron shivered.

They sat in silence then, Aaron pressing back against the chair. He felt sick. Maybe it was the early hour, or the cigarette, or the mole in the complex. He was sure the mole was Gideon. Now he was going to have to save his man over Gideon's objections. The battle would be soon.

Gideon took another breath of smoke.

They sat almost companionably for a few minutes, no conversation. Then the lights from the outer room flooded through the doorway, and the shadows sank under the furniture as low voices drifted without. Aaron stood up and walked to Gideon's door.

Landau hadn't seen him yet. He stood with his crutches fifteen feet away at the desk outside his office talking to his secretary, an unshaved thirtyish sergeant who had obviously just been summoned out of bed. The secretary flipped through a stack of papers as he nodded. Landau was walking better, Aaron noticed, and then Landau looked up and caught Aaron's eye.

"Reuven," the base commander said. "Where's Shimon?"

Aaron gestured behind him. "Here. We're ready, sir."

"Right. Let's go. My office."

Aaron glanced around the base commander's office as Landau waved them to two chairs near his desk. The room was big as offices in the complex went, fifteen feet by twelve, but with little ornamentation. Two detailed maps of Jerusalem—modern and first century—were side by side on one wall. Opposite was a three by five foot schematic of the time machine complex. There was a wall safe behind the desk, the high bookshelf next to it crammed with books on nuclear physics, military tactics, ancient history, and governmental documents. Optical discs lined an entire shelf. The private bathroom door nearby was closed. The only unusual object was a reproduction of a first century oil lamp, resting on top of the small refrigerator in the corner.

The secretary appeared in the doorway. "Sir, the doctor's on the line."

Landau looked up. "Thank you, Hod. Put her on speakerphone in here, then shut the door."

"Yes, sir."

The doctor reviewed the situation. The unconscious soldier, Hirsch, was stable but needed urgent medical care outside their facility, in Jerusalem.

"Do we break the seal over the base?" Landau asked after the doctor had hung up.

"Absolutely not," Gideon said. "The time machine is running. We can't risk its going out of phase with the past. And with a mole present we can't risk unknown personnel gaining access to the base."

Aaron shook his head. "That won't happen. The pilot and the doctor return immediately. No one else goes out or in."

"There's a seal for a reason!" Gideon snapped. "You're the chief of security. You should know this. We don't know what might happen, and FlashBack is critical."

"It's my considered opinion that we can do this safely."

Landau shifted in his chair.

Aaron sat forward. "There's a moratorium on outside communications, so they wouldn't know we're coming. The only people who might even know about the possibility of breaking the seal, General, are the doctor, two medics, two of my security people, your secretary, and us. It's early in the morning. We could be out and back before anyone knew it."

Gideon snorted. "So could a bomb planted on the underside of the helicopter, or an enemy if the security code were tracked. The point is, you can't guarantee anything."

Aaron locked eyes with Landau. "General, I need to question him. He was beginning to draw his gun before the saboteur jumped him."

"What?" Landau asked.

"Yes, sir. I have the visual right here."

Landau tapped his forefinger on the desk. "Shimon, what was going on in that interrogation?"

Gideon shifted in his chair. Aaron wasn't sure, but he thought Gideon gave Landau an almost imperceptible shake of his head.

Aaron sat up. "I suggest we view the recording now."

"Sir," Gideon said to Landau, "may I speak with you privately for a moment first?"

Aaron's ears burned.

Landau looked up. "Yes, of course, Shimon."

Aaron glanced at Gideon, who had the ghost of a smile on his lips.

"You don't mind, do you, Reuven? Why don't you set up the recording in Conference Room A, and we'll be right in."

Aaron flashed through his options. He had no choice. He gritted his teeth. "Of course."

He deliberately left the door to the office open. Keep watch, he thought as he passed the secretary behind the front desk. Surely, Gideon wouldn't be so bold as to try anything now.

He had a bad feeling as he stalked away.

CONCLUSION

You've just learned powerful techniques to amplify tension throughout your story. To summarize, you've seen:

• The difference between Inner and Outer Story, and why you must include an Outer Story to have story tension.

• The three story components: Goal, Stakes, and Obstacles, and how they steer story tension.

• 13 general techniques that ramp story tension:

— Ticking Clock

— Use a Mirror Character to Demonstrate Danger

— Make a Personal Threat

— Take Away Something Important

— Add a Character with a Conflicting Goal

— Add a Positive for Not Completing the Goal

— Close Options

— Exploit the Unknown

— Make the Situation Worse than Previously Thought

— Throw in a Stunning Surprise

—Use Indirect or Confrontational Dialogue

—Keep it Short

—Keep the Problems Coming

• An amazing five minute preplanning step that automatically develops tension in your writing.

• How to build a Scene that incorporates a gripping forward story arrow into your narrative.

• How to build a Sequel that emotionally bonds your reader to your characters.

❋

Please feel free to use the contact form on my website at www.amydeardon.com if you have any questions or comments. I'd love to hear from you!

Thanks so much for reading my book on developing story tension. If you found the information valuable, I hope you'll consider writing a review on Amazon, and/or recommending this to your writing friends on social media.

Happy writing!

TIP SHEET

Tip #1: Make sure you include an external story line (Outer Story) in your narrative. The external line should include a Story Goal, Story Stakes, and Story Obstacles.

———

Tip #2: Make sure your Story Goal is specific, and preferably something physical. The Story Goal's attainment or lack thereof by the end of the story can be decisively answered with a "yes" or "no."

———

Tip #3: Make your Story Stakes important to your hero so they become important to your reader.

———

Tip #4: Your hero should want to accomplish something altruistic by achieving the Story Stakes.

———

Tip #5: To maintain tension always keep at least one story element unknown or uncertain. Use internal and external Story Obstacles to keep the outcome of each action in doubt.

———

Tip #6: Make sure every event that happens in your story puts your hero in a worse position than he was in before the event. Avoid the "One Darn Thing After Another Syndrome" in which your hero's story position is essentially unchanged after the particular event.

———

Tip #7: A ticking clock is an amazingly effective way to add tension for actions both big and small.

———

Tip #8: Portray your hero as competent and likeable (he is funny, friendly, and performs "pet the puppy" actions in which he serves others).

———

Tip #9: A mirror character is someone similar to your hero, and can be used to demonstrate consequences of what may happen when the antagonist attacks someone. Often the harm occurs to the mirror character because he made a wrong choice.

———

Tip #10: Real danger pointed at your hero or, better yet, those close to him, ramps up story tension.

———

Tip #11: On what is your hero relying—a person, information, a tool? Take it away!

Tip #12: Another character with a conflicting goal naturally opposes your hero. An effective means to ramp emotional tension is to make an ally into this oppositional character.

———

Tip #13: Add a positive reason why your hero might not want to pursue his scene goal.

———

Tip #14: Close your hero's options: if he chooses to do something, he will no longer be able to do an equally worthy alternative.

———

Tip #15: Don't reveal all your cards for your story—generate suspense by letting your reader worry about unanswered questions.

———

Tip #16: Reserve a bad surprise for your hero: something is worse than he thought it was.

———

Tip #17: A bad surprise that stuns your hero is good for ramping up tension.

Tip #18: Dialogue is not like real speech. Real speech is full of "umms," circling ideas, and pointless phrases (Hi, how are you? Good, and you?). Dialogue in fiction should contain the quality of verisimilitude—the appearance of reality—while remaining focused, efficient, and progressing through a specific (authorial) agenda.

———

Tip #19: Dialogue can contain great irony and indirect tensions that glue your reader to the story.

———

Tip #20: Deliberately shortening your prose in tense scenes adds an extra punch to your words.

———

Tip #21: Make your chapters short so they read quicker. This technique lures your reader to find out "just one more thing" in your story before taking a break.

———

Tip #22: Most of the Outer Story is a series of actions and reactions—a problem is solved, and another takes its place. To push the story arrow forward, you need to constantly add new problems so your hero's quest to solve his story goal brings constant change and enlightenment. Make the Story Obstacles of different kinds: a need to escape a location for one, a logistical problem, and then an emotional confrontation. Remember that the solution of each Story Obstacle should leave your hero in a different, usually worse place than when he started.

———

Tip #23: To prevent Meandering Story you need to make sure that all the actions in your story, and especially your Outer Story, are building upon and leading to something. Include all the steps you need, and eliminate the side trails.

———

Tip #24: The novel is made up of beads of Scene-Sequel-Scene-Sequel from beginning to end. The purpose of the scene is to clearly articulate the outer story action so that your reader can easily follow story events. The sequel serves to describe your characters' inner emotions and thus increase reader bonding with them and with your story outcome.

———

Tip #25: Each scene must have a purpose and must advance your story in some way. Avoid pointless events, excess verbiage, explanations, background, and rabbit trails.

———

Tip #26: Each scene can only be told through one character's point of view (POV). All observations and emotions in one scene are from the perspective of your POV character. You may switch POV characters for different scenes.

Tip #27: The Inner Story interprets emotions and "inner journeys" and can well tolerate indirect statements and ironic or unstated conclusions. In contrast, the Outer Story statements describing action in story events should be unambiguous since the Outer Story is the framework for everything else.

———

Tip #28: State your scene goal or scene question in one sentence, and use it to start your scene. This goal must be answered clearly with a "yes" or "no" by the end of the scene.

———

Tip #29: Scene Conflict takes up the major part of your scene. It features your hero striving for his Scene Goal while being held back by obstacles. Scene Obstacles can be both internal and external.

———

Tip #30: Scene Obstacles are usually answered sequentially, not interwoven. This makes writing the scene easier.

———

Tip #31: If you wish to increase tension, you may list some hero-known obstacles at the beginning of your scene before your hero starts sequentially dealing with them.

Tip #32: Make sure you're not adding Obstacles simply to add Obstacles. They need to be real problems that take ingenuity to solve. This is what makes story fun.

———

Tip #33: You must answer your scene question, but in such a way that the answer leads to a new scene question. The "Yes, But" answer gives an affirmative, but also a negative consequence. The "No, and Furthermore" answer tells your reader that your hero failed in his scene goal, and this failure has made his situation even worse.

———

Tip #34: Make sure the new scene goals are the result of your hero's actions or another cause you have previously set up. Bad things should not just fall from the sky.

———

Tip #35: The Sequel brings your reader emotionally closer to your characters by having her understand what they think and how they react to story events. Sequel can be one line or full-blown. These are easy to forget to include, so make sure you have them.

———

Tip #36: When your character breaks away after a Scene Disaster, the first thing he does is to emotionally react to the stunning bad news. These emotions aren't logical, simply felt. Some common ones are fear, anger, worry, or grief.

———

Tip #37: After your hero deals with emotions, he must determine his options. List them clearly, with pros and cons for each one. Try to introduce two or more bad options, with no good ones.

———

Tip #38: After clearly reflecting on all his options, your hero should state his decision in one clear sentence. This statement goes either at the end of the sequel, and/or at the beginning of the next scene.

———

Tip #39: After stating his decision, your hero figures out the first thing he needs to do to take action. This start-of-action may be at the very end of your sequel, or at the start of your next scene.

———

Tip #40: By taking five minutes before writing each scene or sequel to clearly articulate why you're including it and where it is headed, you will automatically generate a powerful forward story arrow that your reader will love.

Tip #41: To write your scene, include the following small outline at the top of your blank page:

POV:

GOAL:

CONFLICT:

DISASTER:

———

Tip #42: To write your sequel, include the following small outline at the top of your blank page:

POV:

EMOTION;

THOUGHT;

DECISION:

ACTION:

Even if you don't write a long sequel, it's helpful to do this exercise so you can understand how your characters are responding to your story events.

OTHER BOOKS BY THE AUTHOR

THE STORY TEMPLATE: Conquer Writer's Block Using the Universal Structure of Story

Writing a novel or screenplay sounds like a fabulous idea. But where do you start? And how do you finish?

Award-winning author, Amy Deardon, answers these questions in *The Story Template: Conquer Writer's Block Using the Universal Structure of Story*. This approach will help you focus your creativity and complete your unique and compelling story, script, or novel. With this tool and more than 100 targeted writing exercises, you will learn to:

• Ascertain the four foundational story pillars, and use the "secret weapon" of the story template, to structure your story.

• Build character depth with believable change.

• Create subplots to raise tension while you deepen and contrast story themes.

• Review writing techniques that shape your ideas into a compelling manuscript.

The Story Template is a product of Amy's comprehensive research—as well as her personal experience—for what makes a story "work." No matter your level of accomplishment, this book will help you build a better story.

A LEVER LONG ENOUGH

A small military team travels back in time to film the theft of Jesus' body from the tomb.

In the near future, the Israeli military has developed a prototypic time machine. When believers in Yeshua (Jesus) create a politically explosive situation that threatens the balance of peace between Israel and nearby countries, the Israelis must send a team of four elite soldiers back to film the theft of Jesus' body from the tomb and thus disprove Christianity. The team, consisting of a Special Forces soldier as leader, an ex-American astronaut as engineering specialist, an archaeologist, and a linguist, has exactly seventy-two hours to collect the video evidence.

Drawn into a web of first century deception and death, the only way to escape is for the team to change the past. In the present, a traitor attempts to sabotage the mission and seize control of the military complex. The Special Forces leader operating in the past is the only one who can reveal him, but he is trapped two thousand years away.

Even with a time machine, time is running out.

And from Amy's publisher, Taegais Publishing LLC
(**www.taegais.com**)…

MORTIS by Hannah Cobb

A young assassin must betray all she knows.

In an underground school rife with duels and deadly classes, Jane hides in the shadows to stay alive. She is the invisible assassin. But as she prepares to graduate from Mortis and take her place in the world as a fully-trained killer, Jane stumbles over shadowy secrets revealing dark truths that affect more than her world. Will she embrace the darkness, or betray the school that raised her—and the boy she loves? Once Jane sets herself against her school, there is no turning back because in Mortis, failure always means death.

ABOUT THE AUTHOR: HANNAH COBB lives in Maryland, where she maintains a cover identity as a librarian while moonlighting as a writer. When she isn't writing, Hannah enjoys designing elaborate period costumes and collecting swords. Mortis is her first novel.

SELF-PUBLISH YOUR BOOK—PRINT AND EBOOK FORMATS

Cover Design and E-Book Formatting by EBook Conversion and Listing Services: **www.ebooklistingservices.com**

(a subsidiary of Taegais Publishing LLC—**www.taegais.com**)

❋

PRINT AND E-BOOKS

Self-Publish your book (print and e-format) on Amazon.

Flat low one-time price. No surprise fees, ever.

You always keep full control of your work and all profits.

What we do: Perfect formatting. Interior design. Cover creation. Account set-up. Book listing. Marketing help.

100% satisfaction guarantee or your money cheerfully refunded.

❋

We treat you the way we want to be treated…